NLP

Learn The Art Of Body Language Analysis And How To Defeat Mind Control, Brainwashing, And Deception

(Using Hypnosis, Mind Control, And Other Dark Arts To Persuade Others)

Eugene Burgess

TABLE OF CONTENT

The Model Of NLP Communication 1

We Have The Ability To Modify Our Emotions 11

Fundamentals Of Natural Language Processing 39

Distinguish Between Yourself And Your Behavior 46

Characteristics Of Preferential Manipulator Victims 77

Life Guidance, Mentoring, Evaluation, And Therapy 92

Five Intentions For Hypnosis 110

The Model OfNLP Communication

According to this paradigm, people's behaviour is always repeating itself. And their external behaviour triggers an interior reaction. The person then reacts in a particular way due to the internal reaction. It's thought that an external habit triggers an equivalent inside reaction. As was previously said, the N.L.P. system is thought to show that all exterior habits are typically the result of sensory system experiences. This encompasses the senses of taste, smell, touch, hearing, and vision.

This implies that the senses always trigger every internal reaction that results in certain behaviours. Any internal reaction from an outside habit involves several internal states and internal processes. These are the various ways that sensory experiences might be expressed. Internal processes include things like inner monologue, self-talk, and mental noises. Furthermore, an internal state is the experiences, feelings, and emotional expressions.

The Common N.L.P. Techniques

In N.L.P., strategies are everything. Internal and external habits are involved, and planned strategies for the habits and their reactions are used. It uses various strategies and models to describe human behaviour and how it might be altered. The majority of N.L.P. techniques and tactics are applied temporarily. Established tactics are employed, and their normal and consistent application is contingent upon the situation.

Creating Models

It is thought that modelling served as the inspiration for the N.L.P. theory. This is the method for determining a person's beliefs, similar to physiology. It also refers to the comprehension of individuals' thought processes and tactics. And eventually influences other people's conduct, thoughts, and overall demeanour. It's typically used to identify the methods and actions of the individual that are mentally impacting them, as well as to comprehend the patterns adopted and strategies employed to fulfil assigned functions and responsibilities. This is the case, for example, when someone learns a new language or ability.

According to the approach, one seeking to acquire a new language needs to be aware of three things:

They must be familiar with and comprehend the terminology being utilized.

Understanding and learning the syntax is the second step. At this point, a person may combine all the words to form a phrase.

Understanding mouth or lip movements is the final model. This is a result of the fact that every language has a unique mouth movement and pronunciation. And what he manages to do is to grasp that and communicate with clarity.

The theory makes it abundantly evident that all habits contain the models. There is a high chance of change when you fully comprehend every behavioural pattern in every model. As an illustration, suppose you are at work, and you are unhappy with how you respond to emails. If you're unsatisfied, now is a good time to investigate the response model. Make changes to what you find objectionable about it and search for a more appealing and productive one.

The N.L.P. Strategy: Internal and External

The primary focus of N.L.P. techniques is exposure, both external and internal. Every experience yields well-known results. Regardless of the order, a defined product is always achieved for both internal and external experiences. Getting the greatest results becomes challenging when the sequence and flow are altered. For example, to receive a response to an email you wrote, you must use all of your established internal and external communication experience. Additionally, all planned outcomes won't be successful if the technique is altered.

It always uses a variety of senses, including the gustatory, kinesthetic, aural, visual, and olfactory, to get into all the techniques. It's possible to initiate the outward habit of responding to emails, which might create an inside experience and a particular perception. As a result, some habits will develop. It's crucial to remember that the sensory experiences mentioned above can occur both inside and outwardly. For instance, an N.L.P. therapist will constantly discuss your internal and external experiences during the session. And what they do is make sure that the tactics that are employed are better understood.

The Model of T.O.T.E.

Brandler and Grinder, the creators of N.L.P., also discussed another paradigm called T.O.T.E. This model, which elaborates on how someone else will interpret information, employs many N.L.P. methodologies. T.O.T.E. stands for "Test, Operate, Test, and Exit". This tactic connects to a book by Miller, Pribram, and Galanter, although it largely relates to Bandler and Grinder.

One reacts because the model was used to measure the processes. It determines what primarily sets a habit apart from any strategy. It examines how the strategy is initiated and whether the process repeats itself when tested. For instance, encouraging oneself to compose emails or what first spurred you to pick up the pen. Subsequently, that serves as the trigger, initiating the test and ultimately determining whether or not to begin the writing technique.

The operation, which examines the internal and external procedures required for the strategy to begin and continue, is included in the model. An additional test is conducted to determine the trigger and the initiated process. Next, ascertain whether the habit and tactical approach in the first test were the same. When the exit strategy is effective, it will be revealed. If not, it's important to determine whether the experiences were the same or different from those in the second phase of the operation and whether the trigger was right.

Let's examine a few real-world instances of this.

An illustration involving fear.

For fifty years, a woman in her fifties suffered from a fear of bridges. She was unable to use escalators, glass-sided elevators, or balconies. She recalled being enthralled with water as a toddler and being afraid to release a fence she grasped during that moment of heightened awareness.

While on vacation in Spain, she realized she had to try again to overcome her phobia when she had to get down on all fours to cross a bridge. Her past attempts to overcome this dread had not resulted in any relief.

At about 11.30 a.m., I guided her through this procedure known as a V-K dissociation. That same day, at 3.30 p.m., she ENJOYED crossing a bridge while holding packages.

An instance where a trauma occurred.
A cold-blooded man came to see me. He would have to quit working every year as Winter approached because his head would become extremely cold and numb. Interestingly, he could recall the day and time it began. In a

single session, the V-K dissociation pattern resolved it.

A fear of aeroplanes.
A man who had a severe fear of flying came to visit me. He had not flown on an aeroplane before and had no specific memories. I hypothesized that he had a single meme that supported an imagined scenario in which he was afraid to fly. Using the imagined event as if it were real, this showed to be no exception to the general rule that aeroplane phobias respond well to the V-K dissociation.

A trauma from an automobile accident.
An hour or so earlier, a young woman had been in an automobile accident. It was evident to the witness that the police car had jumped the traffic signals because it was the other vehicle. She was shivering and quite upset. She smiled briefly after using the V-K with a single

separation (in the movie theatre, not the projection room).

The V-K can occasionally help with relatively complex phobias. It's easy to do and frequently worthwhile. In general, agoraphobia and claustrophobia are complex disorders.

It is always important to pay attention to your thoughts when visualizing the problem experience, the phobic or traumatic incident, before performing the V-K (or any other intervention).

What self-talk are you engaging in?

First, the most typical item individuals notice is a statement about their feelings, such as "I feel scared." You're not listening to that. The meme is what you're listening for. Common memes include "I'm being stupid," "Nobody cares anyway," "I've failed again," "It's not fair," and "I don't want to do this."

Pay attention to many ones.

Then, locate the concept in which part of your mind. Typically, different memes occupy distinct locations. The "voice" can occasionally be found outside of the body entirely, or it can sometimes be found inside the body instead of the head.

Once you've finished, swap out the original meme for an affirmative one, like "Life is great," "I persevere and I succeed," or any other positive statement you choose. For every original meme, replace it with a new one.

We Have The Ability To Modify Our Emotions

Individuals are free to alter their emotions whenever they choose. Whether it is because they had introspection and decided to change or because someone else suggested it to them, this is occasionally a manipulative technique used to influence and sway others.

For instance, a person may live their entire life without considering whether or not their sibling borrowed their clothes. One day, though, they'll lose it over the sibling taking clothes and become enraged over something else entirely. Although there are many relationships where this strategy is used, this is just one small example.

While many emotions can be difficult to overcome, some will take these sentiments and try how far they can push them. Our feelings are prone to altering as we age because our meaning and worldview begin to shift at that point.

It is important to note that individuals will experience and transform these emotions in different ways; not everyone will do it in the way that we believe is appropriate. Some people never change or only slightly alter and carry the same emotions throughout their lives. However, some will alter things once a week or more, making it difficult to stay current. It is typically something in between these two for the majority of folks.

Like any other animal, humans enjoy comfort and will look for it. They are terrified of what would happen; thus, they don't want to constantly alter their opinions or some of their deeply held views. Sometimes, this results in unsafe and destructive behaviour, and other times, it results in unhealthy routines that impede the person's ability to grow personally.

Some people might discover that altering their emotions is simple, while others might realize that trying to think or alter one's ideas in any manner is crippling. You will encounter people at all extremes of the spectrum, and each one will be unique. However, this type of independence is beautiful because of it. When it comes to making changes, you have a say. It might be challenging to evolve when we cling to our ideas and opinions for an extended period. However, there is a possibility that we may change, and that change will be positive, and that is the beauty of using NLP techniques.

This chapter has made multiple references to sadists because people who exhibit Dark Triad tendencies can exhibit sadistic conduct. Perhaps you have even come across a sadist once or twice in your life. Perhaps they are still a part of your life. A sadist is someone you know who would deliberately hurt someone else's feelings and get a lot of pleasure from it.

A sadist's activities can range from mild to severe, which is what makes them dangerous.

Typical instances of sadistic conduct include the following:

Using false or unflattering information about another person to harm their reputation; repeating secrets that they know should be kept private; trying to undermine a colleague's reputation behind their back; marginalizing a coworker, friend, family member, or even acquaintance; attempting to break up with someone else; using bullying or cyberbullying; stealing intellectual, material, or financial property.

A competent sadist will manipulate these circumstances so precisely that it will be challenging to establish that they were the guilty party. Even worse, they have no intention of accepting responsibility or feeling regret for the harm they have caused. Because of their endearing and likeable characteristics, people could even find it hard to accept that the sadist is the cause of the mayhem.

A sadist will go out of their way to purposefully hurt someone else because they think it would help them. They may use these devious methods whenever they feel threatened or jealous of someone else or even think the other person is weaker and less inclined to strike back. There are situations in which it is unclear why the sadist has decided to assault the victim. Although it's not something we frequently consider or want to accept, sadists can exist in our immediate social circles. These include your parents, siblings, spouse, extended relatives, friends, and coworkers.

Here's an example of a situation where a sadist could be present in your household. Assume that John Smith, the individual, recently lost his job and was experiencing worry and frustration due to his difficulty finding a new one. John talks to his brother about it to get support and consolation, but he clearly wants his brother to keep the information to himself. John's sibling concurs. After some time, John receives an invitation for a laid-back get-together at his brother's house. John is then shocked, not thinking much of it, when several people express their condolences for losing his job and being unable to find another.

John, feeling embarrassed, wounded, and furious, realizes right away that his brother was the one who disclosed his secret because he hadn't shared his problems with anyone else. Later on, when John confronts him, his brother says he "has no idea" what John is talking about and denies having any knowledge of it. John feels bad for thinking he is the guilty party because his brother is still vehemently disputing the charges. It takes John some time to realize that he and his brother had encountered this identical problem before when John's brother denied any responsibility for several incidents that have left John feeling hurt or embarrassed.

The sadist can be anybody, anywhere, and they always hide in the shadows, making you doubt your sanity. At the same time, they intentionally cause you pain and suffering in your life while rejecting any sort of accountability.

Psychopathy

It's difficult to define psychopathy exactly, but it's generally understood to be a mental illness marked by impulsivity, superficial appeal, and a loss of typically "Human" emotions like empathy and regret. A person with these qualities who is well-known is called a psychopath. Some of the most dangerous people on the globe are psychopaths; they are wolves in sheep's clothes.

People might identify the word "psychopath" with the image of a crazy guy with a mask on and a machete. The reality is horrifying.

Appropriate psychopaths are more likely to be the attractive, alluring outsider who wins their victims over before destroying or perhaps terminating their lives.

It's interesting to note that some of the top names routinely score exceptionally well on psychopathy persona tests; they are in the business field. The general public increasingly perceives psychopathy as a social problem rather than a personal one for those who exhibit it. Because they are no longer restrained by using the sympathetic indecision that most people enjoy, psychopaths are frequently able to achieve success in any field they choose, whether it is finance or serial killing.

Psychopathic Behavior

You possess comprehensive knowledge of the basic traits of psychopathy and what sets real psychopaths apart from those in popular culture. You won't be able to identify someone as a psychopath based only on theoretical knowledge unless you are a trained psychotherapist with close contact with them. On the other hand, it is critical to recognize the external signs of psychopathy as those are typically the greatest ways to identify psychopathy behaviour before it is much too late.

One of the most typical exterior characteristics of a psychopathic persona is physical attraction. That's important to understand, but it's not true allure; it's just surface appeal. If you reflect on a charming individual in your own life, you'll probably find that their amazing personality growth undermined their external behaviours. Should this kind of obviously alluring guy or woman's captivating behaviour truly be an act of charity and a desire to bring happiness to people? In the case of a psychopath, this is untrue.

Mendacity is just another trait that distinguishes psychopaths. It is insufficient in and of itself to place a person in the diagnostic category of psychopathy. However, when paired with other traits, it may suggest a psychopathic identity. For a psychopath, lying is as normal as breathing for those with very stable minds. A psychopath can deceivingly present the truth as something else at any given time. Psychopaths lack emotional attachment to their falsehoods and do not experience shame, guilt, or joy when they lie, which is another reason why they do not exhibit the telltale signs and symptoms of lying. Mendacity to psychopaths is just "doing what is wanted at the time."

Another characteristic that sets psychopaths apart from non-psychopathic people is a lack of regret. Many people who have committed horrible crimes, such as murder, suffer from intense feelings of guilt and shame over what they have done. Some of these people have even committed suicide as a result of these feelings. Psychopaths aren't inherently incapable of feeling regret; it's only that it takes longer for them to feel it. Seeking regret from a psychopath is like asking a deaf person to focus on song lyrics.

A lack of guilt is closely linked to a lack of remorse. When someone violates a few different personal ethical standards, they typically experience guilt. Guilt is foreign to psychopaths since they perceive things not in terms of right and wrong but rather as beneficial or no longer beneficial. The closest explanation for a psychopath's feelings of guilt or regret is the conviction that their actions did not meet their standards for what constitutes a suitable psychopath.

Another distinguishing feature of psychopathy is a lack of impulse control. Most humans possess internal restraints and defence systems that keep them from acting rashly. These defence mechanisms are absent in psychopaths. A psychopath will act without hesitation or consideration of the second principle if they find an opportunity they wish to take advantage of. This could be raping someone they want to rape, killing someone they want to kill, or stealing something they want. Because of their vicious impulses, psychopaths are among the most cunning individuals in industries like business and the military. Many non-psychopaths lack the instinctive impulse to act decisively, and to be honest, this deficiency is detrimental to advancement in lifestyles.

Psychopaths are completely devoid of any form of empathy. Psychopaths don't see anyone who isn't like them as real or valuable at all. They resemble badly sketched stick figures on paper. Beyond what they can provide for the psychopathic man or woman, their lives are worthless and of no use. When a psychopath witnesses a terrible event, their first thought is usually, "How does this affect me? How can I take advantage of this for myself? Rather than any kind of sincere reaction in any way.

Additional characteristics of dark psychology

In addition to the four primary characteristics of dark psychology, other features are strongly associated with those above four. Among them are:

The fixation with one's accomplishments at the detriment of others is known as egoism. They minimize others' accomplishments and consider themselves the greatest in their profession, even if they are comparable to or even greater than them. They take pride in what they have accomplished and ignore that of others.

Moral Disengagement: Individuals with dark psychological personalities may act unethically without feeling guilty. They believe their acts have no repercussions and that they can offend anyone.

Psychological entitlement: an individual possessing these characteristics feels better than others regarding their actions, ideas, and disposition.

People who exhibit dark psychological features tend to be bitter and think that getting even is the right thing to do. They don't care who suffers as long as they exact revenge, even if it is themselves.

Machiavellian thought

Machiavellianism is a psychological term for a personality characteristic indicating an individual is completely preoccupied with their interests. These people carelessly deceive, manipulate, and exploit their victims to fulfil their ambitions. Niccolò Machiavelli, a notable

Renaissance philosopher, is the source of the word Machiavellianism. He penned a book outlining his opinions on how strong leaders should interact with their people. He thought powerful leaders treated their opponents and subjects harshly and that anyone might achieve glory and survival by doing anything, no matter how cruel or unethical.

It is discovered that men are more likely than women to exhibit Machiavellianism in dark psychology. But it can affect anyone, including young ones.

One of the most well-known NLP instructors teaches guys how to use NLP-based techniques to elicit positive feelings in people of the opposite gender and increase their chances of having a meaningful, fulfilling experience. The techniques centre on a few quite arcane concepts, such as creating a positive internal state that can be transferred to the other person via the law of state transference. The ideas underlying this and the methods for finishing it are explained in detail in the book's later enchantment section.

The models shown here represent some of NLP's more reliable and acceptable applications in people's lives. The following section of this piece will demonstrate how these ideas might be rethought in an uninteresting way that draws on human weakness to influence and subtly affect others. It should be noted that ideas such as these exist on the periphery of the NLP community; they are not widely accepted or even aware of. These are the obscure mysteries in the field of NLP that will typically be revealed for the first time.

The Saddest NLP Instances from Real Life

Based on this area of influence, one uninteresting application of NLP has been in schools of temptation. While most people use the principles of NLP to improve their chances of succeeding in dating by doing so conventionally and sufficiently, a few marginal personalities have committed themselves to promoting hazily decimating applications for NLP lessons. It is advised that you continue reading cautiously because the ideas accompanying them could be harmful in the wrong hands.

Typically, patterns are used to hint at the subtle NLP techniques that are used as enticement. A series of instances gained notoriety in the enchantment community and were dubbed the forbidden examples. They got this term because, in the community, they were too gloomy and superficial for anyone to take seriously. The local community has looked for them a lot due to their reputation, but they are hard to find. Here is a complete introduction to them.

"The Shadow and the Rising Sun" is one example. It is typically forbidden within the enticing region due to its utilization of Jungian brain science concepts to reveal a woman's hidden side or shadowy aspect of her psyche.

The tempter achieves this by initiating a conversation on contrasts. He focused on continuously examining how to distinguish symbols that can reveal the potential for ambiguity, such as yin and yang and light and dull. He talks about how everything is meaningless without a dark side, a basic aspect of life. Then, he starts discussing how everyone has a dark side. This should be apparent given the chance of a rising sun, which casts shadows and significantly alters everyone's perspective. Then, the enticer invites the goal to enter her clouded side and see the world from its point of view. The goal is to put the target in a situation where they are susceptible and respond differently than they normally would.

Another often-used method is the medical clinic design to the strategy above. In this instance, the enticer alternates between his target's exuberant feelings of excessive pleasure and outrageous anguish. This abrupt shift in intense emotions, which fluctuate frequently, is anticipated to make the target predisposition impulsive and, therefore, unaffected. When the target is in this state of vulnerability, the enticer can anchor the target's sense of happiness to himself and their sense of pain to an alternative. By doing this, the tempter ensures the target has a tremendous sense of joy associated with the enticer, who can trigger these feelings at will.

A thing known as an example intrusion is another nefarious application of NLP going after temptation. Here, the tempter uses Dark NLP to lessen her levelheadedness, protect instruments, and stop his target from achieving what he doesn't require. For example, the tempter might ask her something completely unrelated, like, "What's your cherished shading?" if the target begins to rattle off a litany of reasons why she shouldn't be with the enticer. The enticer upsets the target's viewpoint in this way, which leads to guard instruments. This prevents the goal from adopting its recurring tendencies.

Additionally, NLP has been duly applied to cause people to doubt whether their memories are real and which are made up. There is a tactic where the goal is put in a relaxing state frequently likened to being between being awake and asleep. The goal is quite suggestible in this expression. The goal is to guide them backwards through their memories until the Dark NLP client notices a memory they want to disturb. After that, they pose a series of queries meant to cast doubt on the target's recollection and make them wonder whether it was all in their head. This can undermine the target's sense of self and cause them to doubt their beliefs and ideals of who they are. This is often the first stage in programming someone to assume a new identity.

A similar process can be applied to implant false memories that are perceived as real in the brain of an objective. Just like in the previous process, the target is put into a state of deep relaxation where they are rendered immune to influence. After that, they are transported back through their memories. When the time is right, a series of probing questions are used to try and get the subject to remember something that never happened.

Asking the target questions like "Then do you remember when x happened?" and "How did you feel when x happened?" usually starts with a genuine recollection. The latter form of the question directs the target's mental attention toward evoking an emotional reaction. The mind expects the occasion to be true since it is presented as a fact rather than a claim. This is used to resurrect memories of events that never occurred, as in the case of cult members who trick their victims into believing they were abused by their parents when none of it ever happened. This is a common technique for separating an object from its surroundings.

The NLP Controversy

It has been shown that NLP is among the least reliable subfields within brain science. Now, we'll go into various conversations that NLP has generated and explore the reasons behind the standard's disapproval and unease with this field. By doing this, the power of NLP will be clearly defined and presented in a way that highlights how much more than just basic knowledge NLP—particularly Dark NLP—is.

Several NLP's initial responses originated inside the traditional brain research calling. Conventional experts and practitioners raised concern about NLP's dangers since it sought quicker ways to achieve outcomes that were only possible with delayed, traditional treatment. According to the experts, going for these quicker methods suggested that people weren't healed but had learned to conceal their wounds more deeply. The world of NLP retaliated, stating that the demand for brain research was only increased because the slow results were becoming less and less sufficient for individual needs. Since the early stages of NLP, there has been a conflict about authenticity.

One topic of contention surrounding NLP is the idea that it empowers immoral behaviour. NLP is perceived as enabling people to act in ways that are harmful and self-centred since it teaches people how to deeply understand and influence others. In response, NLP educators have stated that it is unfair to single out NLP for this kind of scrutiny. Almost every thought process can be used for good or bad, and it is not the fault of anyone other than the individual employing dishonest tactics.

Have faith in yourself.

Your beliefs have a big impact on your behaviour and accomplishments. Your actions will be consistent with your belief that you are incapable of accomplishing anything or useless. You will most likely fail because you are not acting in a way that is favourable to success. However, you will behave with greater confidence and have a higher chance of success if you have self-confidence.

To practice NLP, you must change your beliefs. Give up on negative thinking. Give up thinking that you are unworthy. Rather, think that you are truly talented and skilled and that everything is possible, even if you're not quite ready for a career or competition.

Eliminate any ideas that contain the terms "cannot," "should not," or "not good enough." Substitute them with ideas that begin with "can" or "will." Have faith that everything will work out in due course.

Pose Appropriate Questions

You may start to modify your outlook after you have an understanding of it.

Regretfully, we frequently ask ourselves questions in a way that does not help us feel better. You ask yourself negative questions, which makes you come up with negative responses. These responses simply depress you and draw your attention away from the good and toward what is right.

You should ask questions that make you consider constructive ways to feel or act better rather than doing this. If you can come up with more constructive questions and constructive responses, you can inspire yourself. Asking yourself questions that focus on solutions to your problems rather than just what's wrong with your life is another thing you should do.

For instance, if you have a weight issue, you would ask yourself, "Why am I so fat?" Subsequently, you discover every reason for your obesity and every mistake you make in your way of living. This does not solve your weight problem; it makes you feel worse. But if you ask yourself a different question that makes you consider positive and gain, you may ask yourself, "Why do I want to lose weight?" You'll consider how you want to feel, look, and live longer for your children and grandchildren. Next, ask yourself, "Is there a way I could improve my health and reduce my weight?" You start to come up with pretty concrete fixes. Asking yourself, "Why do I feel so bad?" causes you to consider all the negative aspects of your life and how you have let yourself down. It hardly cheers you up. If anything, it only lowers your mood and decreases your motivation to make changes. Therefore, you ought to pose a more constructive query to yourself, like, "How can I feel better?" And "What will life be like after I feel better?" You'll bring the thought into your head before you see yourself feeling better. Just thinking positively and constructively about it will make you feel better.

Fundamentals Of Natural Language Processing

NLP is a neuro-linguistic program; you must communicate with your neural system to reach your full potential. The network of nerves that runs from your brain to your toes is known as the nervous system. The nerve system is crucial to communication; NLP practitioners refer to these principles as the "essential" or "presupposition" of NLP.

NLP presumption

As we already know, success requires most of the brain's resources. Everyone knows that to succeed, one needs to put in a lot of study time and effort, yet there are numerous formulas for success. According to common belief, putting in more work and energy can help you focus better. While everyone can use a neuro-linguistic program, the key is to identify a catalyst, which is demonstrated by an individual's capacity to apply the fundamentals of NLP. Furthermore, there is a context for every behaviour. A context can be established by saying, "There are two things we will discuss if we have time." We just need to add more stuff. In every facet of life, context and content are crucial. Assume I tell a friend, "Hey, you are a donkey," and I reprimand them. I don't want to hurt him, even though he understands what I mean by saying "donkey." But how I say it indicates that we are still friends even if he made a mistake. I'm not being critical of him. The context would change, but the message would remain the same if I called out a stranger for making a mistake (such as verbally disparaging my way of life without realizing it). NLP is this. As we work through the modules, we'll see more examples and have more discussions afterwards.

The tendency toward aggression in persons is another general norm worth considering.

Put simply, those who are aggressive are afraid. Clearly.

An extremely rigid posture and a typically emotionless facial expression indicate aggressive behaviour. This is meant to tell others that they should not be trifled with. But you can tell if they're a horrible guy or if this is all just posturing.

Psychopaths and other truly evil people are, in fact, extremely pleasant people. How many stories of a pleasant neighbour with a dead body basement have you heard of? The truth is that psychopaths are typically highly intelligent and gregarious people.

Then, some lack self-control and are impetuous. These are the people who behave fearfully. They'll be more likely to resort to violence out of a simple fear that someone else will enter and exploit their weaknesses. These people will become angry easily and start a fight quickly. To put it briefly, it is advisable to avoid them. If you have to deal with them, your best chance is to counteract their aggressiveness with composure and relaxation.

Standing your ground is the greatest course of action when dealing with someone who is essentially bullying. The first to give in within the animal kingdom is typically the one who loses. The same thing happens to us, but it happens on a psychological level.

For instance, exhibiting symptoms of subordination to an overbearing supervisor or superior can encourage them to try to take advantage of you. You don't usually have to prevail in a yelling war with your supervisor. They might later turn the tables on you, after all. You can usually make your point by emerging victorious in a contest of stars. This stems from the reality that bullies are essentially insecure individuals. Thus, simply maintain your ground if interacting with an aggressive person. Most of the time, you won't need to say anything to convey your point.

An excellent general rule of thumb is to know when someone is truly afraid.

Among the worst emotions in the world is fear. It has the potential to render a person paralyzed. They can end up helpless as a result. When you are in a position of power, you may feel pressured to seize the opportunity and force your opponent to play the role of the victim. Even if doing so may help you gain what you want, you can covertly take advantage of people's fear to act as a defender or saviour.

Head down, arms and legs crossed, and evasive eye contact are obvious defensive postures linked to fear. However, there are a ton of additional indicators that you might miss. For instance, people who are afraid will keep quiet and still. This relates to the reaction of fight, flight, or freeze.

You may determine that a fearful person would like to attack first since scared people can become aggressive (fight response). Some become icy under duress. Most aggressors will take advantage of this vulnerable circumstance when it occurs. Attackers can cause severe injuries to someone who is terrified to the point of paralysis.

Now, physical assault is not the only way that this position of control over someone else can manifest itself. When a supervisor goes on a tirade, you'll find that many people at work become astonished and are unable to respond. Sometimes, coworkers go too far, while others cannot handle it. The freeze response is, in fact, arguably the most evident. However, it can be risky since someone cornered may respond in several ways. Therefore, when someone feels cornered, there is an unpredictable element involved.

The flight response comes next. A person may choose to take flight when they are afraid, whether it be from emotional trauma or physical danger. In this response, you can observe actions like avoiding eye contact and excessive fidgeting. If excessive leg movement is seen, it can provide insight into the degree of terror experienced by an individual.

Tilting or turning toward the closest exit is another automatic response to someone who poses a flight risk. They seek the quickest route out of instinct. This can be further supported if you witness someone having their phone in their hand. All they're waiting for is the first opportunity to flee.

The third tenet: Modifying conduct

This idea primarily calls for changing your conduct till you reach your intended outcome. Of course, that may sound easier said than done. Try a different approach if the one you are using isn't working anymore. To determine whether or not what you are doing is goal-oriented, you must use your sensory awareness. If so, feel free to proceed. If not, locate an appropriate replacement.

Your activities toward your intended outcome, regardless of how comfortable or uncomfortable they may be for you, must be guided by how they will affect others and yourself. But it's crucial to remember that you must give up as soon as you reach your objectives—or else you risk making a mess. Furthermore, you must consciously and firmly embrace the result of your circumstances.

Distinguish Between Yourself And Your Behavior

It's critical to separate yourself from your actions. It is not always a sign of failure to fail at something, even though you might fail at it. Your actions, words, or emotions in a given situation determine your behaviour. You are not this. You are far more powerful and expansive than your actions.

Regulation No. 13. Failure is a teaching tool.

You will reach your intended result as you learn to use your life events as a springboard for growth and learning. It just indicates that you have found one method that does not work; failing at anything does not imply failure per se. You must adapt your actions and figure out a strategy that works.

How To Set Goals Using NLP

What are your desires?

Express your desires rather than your dislikes. Put another way, what do you want if X isn't what you're after?

Give specifics. To produce precisely what you want, ensure you know how your goal feels, sounds, and appears. This will assist your unconscious mind in assembling as many tools as possible to support you in reaching your objective.

When, where, and who do you want to help you accomplish your objective? In certain situations, this might be applicable, but not in others. Make sure you mentally rehearse to learn.

Is this a minor result or a major result? To what extent does it align with your core values and beliefs?

What are the estimated dates of your accomplishments?

What difference does it make to you if you succeed in your endeavour? Furthermore, what good will it do for you if you succeed in your goal? Ask yourself these questions multiple times to find out what is more important to you. There may be more effective techniques to achieve your goals than the one you had in mind.

How will you know when your aim has been accomplished?

Give details. When you succeed, what will you see, hear, and experience? Then, what will you be doing, and will anyone else notice the difference?

What signals will indicate that you're getting closer to your objective? Is there a method to demonstrate your improvement in a minor but meaningful way? You may have accomplished a lot without realising it.

Furthermore, how frequently are you going to monitor your progress?

Is there another method to achieve your goals? This is a question you should also ask yourself.

How attainable is your objective?

You can succeed if it has been accomplished by someone else. If you are the first to attempt it, see if it is feasible. This will essentially need doing it! What restricts other people may not limit you. You may find solace in that many significant advancements were originally thought impossible until someone tried them and achieved the seemingly impossible. If you discover that your objective is unachievable, alternative ways exist to attain its significance.

If the objective seems too big, divide it into manageable chunks.

Are your goals within your control to achieve?

Make sure your goals align with the things you have direct control over.

Ensure your outcome consists of what you can do if it involves others. For example, you may wish your employer to be more approachable, but you have no control over their attitudes, behaviours, or sentiments. Nevertheless, as you are the one in charge, you can (a) alter your behaviour to influence your employer to act in the manner that you desire or (b) alter your attitude to reduce the amount of worry that your boss causes you. However, you can also (c) find another employment or (d) try to find a way to reorganise the company so there isn't a boss.

What is preventing you from achieving your goals right now?

Fourth Principle: Authority

It is a common observation that the listener's subconscious mind immediately processes what a powerful person says. When you assert your authority over someone else, they unconsciously accept it.

To help you better grasp how this principle operates, consider the following scenario: you visit your doctor, and they recommend medications, so you go right out and get them. This is as a result of your acceptance that the doctor was the one in charge here. Your thoughts will be preoccupied with the idea of buying the doctor's recommended medications until you do so.

Influential individuals are frequently used in marketing campaigns and other initiatives because they resemble official authorities. It's easier for you to convince others to use your product when they see someone with such a personality using it.

Furthermore, you may have seen that doctors are asked to participate in ads for toothpaste or medications. Advertisers of fitness products invite fitness community members to participate in their campaigns and advertisements. Persuading the other person gets simpler because these individuals are the authoritative figures, and others recognise them as such. This is a widely applied concept in the world.

You must first have confidence in yourself and arm yourself with all the tools an authoritative person would have needed to project an air of authority. It would also be simpler for the other person to accept you as the authority figure and believe you this way. After completing this, you can present your product or service to them. If you can project authority and behave accordingly, you may persuade others to accept your decisions.

When a doctor doesn't act or present themselves as a doctor, your mind will never recognise them as a legitimate authority. Therefore, to convince someone, you must present an authoritative image and provide them with the necessary skills.

Step 2: Understanding Why Mindless Thoughts Are Negative

Understanding the significance of preventing unmindful thoughts is the second step towards comprehending mindfulness. The human mind comprises two parts: the conscious and the subconscious. The latter is an inactive portion, whereas the former is the most active. While the inactive offers us automatic directions, the former facilitates clear thinking.

Our thinking generates both positive and bad ideas. Someone can't think exclusively positively, and even when we consciously try to think positively, our subconscious will still produce and let go of negative ideas.

It's estimated that 70% of our thoughts are negative, leaving us very unhappy. It is also easier said than done, despite our belief that we can control our thoughts and stop unpleasant things from happening.

As we all know, the four noble truths of life never cease to provoke reflection. Even with our best attempts, we find it difficult to escape them. We may, however, exert considerable control over or suppression of them.

We must explore the depths of our subconscious to teach it to think constructively. And if we practise mindfulness, that is achievable.

As is well known, practising mindfulness helps us to be fully present in the moment. This enables us to stop the broad effects of our subconscious mind on us.

It's like saying that your mind won't be able to consider the many ideas since it will be too busy being absorbed. Without a doubt, mindfulness will assist you in this regard, but you should make every effort to prevent it.

Sorting and Storing with NLP

Partitioning is another fantastic way that neuro-linguistic programming is applied to mind control. NLP may be used to build mentally segregated areas that can be deleted or retrieved and to prioritise and arrange ideas and tasks. Remember the visualisation of the clean slate? It's time to clear your head and put everything for later.

After you made mental space, what did you do with the mess? You imagined placing it on shelves or in a filing cabinet drawer. How you clear your mental clutter will influence your memory for information. Visualisation is a terrific tool, whether you're organising your thoughts for the present or the future. To be mentally and physically organised at work, home, and school, it is critical to compartmentalise, prioritise, memorise, and use this skill.

Using NLP visualisation, you may organise and prioritise your ideas. This can be accomplished by visualising your previously created chaotic mental area. All of your ideas and thoughts will materialise inside of you. Now, picture-setting your thoughts aside to declutter your mind. But this time, you'll have to pay attention to the locations and methods of storing your thoughts.

Your closet needs to be arranged similarly to a closet. Organise items you use frequently in a more convenient location. Arranging these notions at "eye level" in your mental archives is best. Spend some time talking to yourself about these things. Say to yourself, "I need this for my project." Okay, that's enough.

Even if the ideas and thoughts you're looking for don't come to you right away, talk to yourself about them. Verify your shelf visualisations by saying, "This event will take place in two weeks," or "I'll file it here so I can get to this soon." You can do this for any foggy thought. You may even picture yourself listing where your belongings are placed in your storage area.

If your ideas are excessively disorganised, you can also sort recollections. You can create mental memory boxes and review each memory as you file it away. Consider how it made you feel and where it's kept if you have a nice memory. You will find it easier to remember the event later if you can remember where it was kept. After you remember the lesson you learnt and your feelings, place the memory in a box and store it in your brain. That way, you won't have to relive the traumatic experience to remember the lesson and your emotions.

Your brain can be more efficiently organised and productive with the help of NLP. It will enable you to clear your mind quietly and consistently and help you become more present with your abilities and memories. Talking to yourself about your ideas and memories can help you picture yourself becoming organised. This will give you the motivation and resources to be more structured outside. This is a crucial step in acquiring NLP and other practical skills. Knowing what matters to you most can help you stay focused and make the required adjustments.

What you preserve as memories and what you put away for later might teach you a lot. You can arrange and store ideas to concentrate on the most crucial problems and tasks. It's important to remember that compartmentalising something doesn't necessarily indicate that you don't value it; rather, it only indicates that you understand when it needs to be placed on hold.

We must identify and then modify the beliefs and actions detrimental to our well-being and impede our progress. Numerous mental health issues, including anxiety, phobias, stress, and even post-traumatic stress disorder, have been effectively treated with NLP.

A growing number of professionals are using NLP for profit, promising increased output and accomplishing work-related goals, which eventually lead to career advancement.

Let's now examine how NLP functions. With his pupil Richard Bandler, John Grinder studied the methods employed by Milton Erickson, the renowned hypnotherapist, Virginia Satir, the family therapist, and Gestalt therapy pioneer Fritz Perls. After that, they simplified and examined these therapeutic approaches to establish a behavioural model that could be widely used to attain and maintain greatness in any field. Bandler, a computer science major, contributed to creating a "psychological programming language" for people.

Our mind creates an internal "NLP map" of the outer world based on how it interprets information and views the outside environment. Our senses—the images we see, the sounds we hear, the taste we taste, the feelings we experience on our skin, and the smells we can detect—provide the input to create this internal map.

However, this enormous information overload makes our minds filter out and generalise much information. Each person makes a different choice based on what their mind thinks is pertinent to the circumstances.

Consequently, we often overlook a great deal of information readily apparent to another person from the outset, leaving us with a limited and distorted picture of what is happening. Take a moment to consider the following statement, for instance: "Person A killed person B." We will have a different version of this tale based on our experiences and circumstances.

Others may believe that "a terrorist killed a baby," "a man killed a woman," "a lion killed a man," "John Doe killed Kennedy," and so on.

There is a method to this craziness, so whatever story you came up with, acknowledge that your experiences influenced it.

The circumstance at hand is internally mapped by our mind, which we then compare to other internally mapped situations from our past that we have mentally stored. Each person has an internal "library" that reflects their personality and what is meaningful or essential to them.

Have you ever thought that the universe is suddenly showing you hints that could lead you to achieve your goals as soon as your conscious mind makes you aware of what you want to accomplish or acquire? For instance, you might wake up one day and decide you and your family must go on vacation.

You continue your day as you have for several days or weeks until suddenly, while driving to work, you see a poster about an exciting trip to Florida. Later, you find out from a coworker that this poster has been up for over a month. You suddenly notice that there is a large travel agency nearby that you had never noticed before, right next to the Starbucks you go to every day.

You'll notice that while you're online, advertisements for travel or accommodations will appear on your YouTube videos or throughout your Facebook feed. All of them may seem like coincidences, but the truth is that those indications or items were there the entire time; you just chose to ignore them since they didn't apply to you.

Thus, as your conscious mind begins to connect your desires and the world, you begin to notice new information that may have been there all along but that you are now becoming aware of.

They believe they won't be discovered.

Another reason people manipulate is because they believe their cunning schemes will go unnoticed, and the targets would not recognise that they are being led astray. Furthermore, they are sure that even if their deception is exposed, the victim won't be able to take any action.

Why do manipulators believe they will escape detection? Some people seem innately naive, timid, fragile, and clueless. These are the individuals that manipulators target. They contend that someone who lacks self-worth, confidence, or knowledge of worldly ways is less likely to recognise when they are being duped.

Additionally, manipulators know that the victim will have few options if their manipulation scheme is discovered. They carefully choose people who lack confidence, self-acceptance, a positive body image, or a sense of value. Playing on these people's weaknesses is simpler than doing so with confident, aggressive individuals who won't let others take advantage of them.

Say someone lacks social awareness, finds jokes difficult to understand, fails to recognise pranks quickly, cannot distinguish between sexual advances and genuine courtesy, is unable to tell if someone is genuinely attracted to them or is just interested in going to bed with them, and exhibits other similar social and interpersonal dynamics. That individual is more susceptible to manipulation.

The fact that victims are powerless to stop their abusers if they remain unaware that their vulnerabilities are being exploited is well-known to manipulators. They frequently take advantage of their victims' ignorance by claiming that they are hallucinating or making things up. A person who is already unsure and uninformed is less likely to challenge this notion. How tough is it for a manipulator to take advantage of your feelings of vulnerability, uncertainty, and cluelessness by adding more reinforcement to them?

Tricksters

The reason manipulators manipulate is that they believe they have more power to hurt or upset their victims than the victims have over them. Those who seem kind and defenceless will nearly always be their target. People aren't truly used to dishonest allegiances when unaware of the dishonesty in social connections. They are less conscious of being influenced because they lack the tools to confront or combat dishonesty.

They Cannot Acknowledge Their Faults.

People naturally tend to minimise other people when they cannot acknowledge their own failings or refuse to take responsibility for them.

The drive to make others feel equally worthless or sad about themselves arises when manipulators feel inadequate or unhappy about themselves. When someone feels unworthy of another person, they manipulate that person into feeling the same way. They can then take charge of their belief that they require the manipulator in their lives to feel deserving. They feel a kind of false superiority when they make fun of others or try to manipulate them. They give others the impression that they are unworthy of their control if they are unable to live up to other's expectations of them.

Essentially, those who manipulate others wish for their victims to never know that they (the manipulators) are inferior to them (the victims). To maintain the victim's attachment to him or her, the manipulator will, therefore, deliberately sow seeds of helplessness and unworthiness in the victim. The more gorgeous, bright, wealthy, capable, efficient, self-sufficient, etc., a person realises about themselves, the more likely they will leave the manipulator. However, if the manipulator instils a sense of incompleteness in the victim, they will require an external source to fulfil them.

Manipulators are unable to take responsibility for their actions or handle criticism. They frequently struggle with complex psychological problems or insecurities. They can feel superior to others without facing their fears by controlling others. Even minor advice, criticism, or correction might feel like a major setback to someone with such a limited viewpoint.

Manipulators cannot accept failure.

Observe how manipulators rarely show their gratitude or thankfulness. Being thankful to others is difficult for them since, in their opinion, it makes them feel more obligated to others, which doesn't provide them an advantage in relationships.

When you give someone a big favour, for instance, they feel obligated to repay you, elevating you above them in the relationship dynamics until they do. The goal of manipulators is not to feel obligated to you and give you the upper hand. They won't show gratitude, making you think you haven't done much for them and they owe you nothing. The whole point is to always outdo you; they don't feel that way because they feel obligated to you.

Instances Of Manipulative Acts

While all of this may seem a bit far-fetched and unreal, manipulative behaviours occur frequently in day-to-day interactions. For example, you wrote a significant file yesterday afternoon and sent it to a coworker so he could review it again and return it to you. However, when you arrived at work this morning, your supervisor was at your desk and yelled at you, accusing you of not writing the file.

Following your boss's tirade, you walked arrogantly over to a colleague, and an odd thing happened: the colleague convincingly claimed that you had never given him the file, which made you start to doubt your recall!

This is an excellent illustration of manipulative behaviour—gas lighting.

Under no circumstances will manipulative people admit guilt; for example, you and your friend got into a fight this week, but after giving it some thought, you decided that your reactions were a little too dramatic.

You decide to make amends by going to your friend's house, but after you apologize and are accepted, you discover that your friend did not extend an apology.

The response would be brief if you asked nicely for it: "No, of course, I don't have to apologize! I wouldn't have become upset if you hadn't done something so foolish."

Naturally, this is illogical thinking that is practically synonymous with deceptive actions.

Saying, "You fell sick this week, and it was so bad that even walking from the bed to the couch was too much trouble," is another excellent example of manipulative behaviour.

You started to feel a little better after a week. Afterwards, when you went to support your son's football game, you told one of the other parents that you were sick and couldn't bring your son to the game. What you expected was not the response you received: "Is that all? Man, that's nothing! Last year, I was so sick that I broke out in bruises on my lungs from coughing so hard, but I still had to go through the queue because you have to be there for your kids. Isn't your parenting excellent?

This was not just a poor response—since you were ill last week and couldn't do it—but also a deceptive one.

The parent had denigrated you in addition to downplaying and emphasizing your issues.

NLP and personal development

NLP treatments and theories are excellent for actualization actualization and self-improvement. Since filters like beliefs, values, and meta-programs can restrict an individual's potential, it makes sense to anticipate that internal representations and emotional states will also shift when these factors shift.

Before moving on, I want to clarify what I mean by self-actualization and self-improvement.

While it is possible to understand better one's bodily or mental well-being as self-improvement, that is not what I mean, as those subjects fall under the areas of NLP applications for physical or mental well-being. Instead, my perspective is extremely close to the one that Abraham Maslow, PhD, advanced when he developed his theory of the Hierarchy of Needs. According to him, people are driven to seek fulfilment at a lower level before moving on to a higher one. In that sequence, His levels are self-actualization, esteem, love/belonging, safety, and physiology.

I only consider the latter two levels of NLP relevant to self-actualization and progress; the other levels are confined to physical and mental health domains. As a result, my concentration is on issues like self-worth, accomplishment, confidence, respect for oneself and others, creativity, and intuition.

Now that I've made this point clear, it is appropriate to mention that the person attempting to employ NLP interventions wants to change from their current situation to what they believe to be their actual potential. Even commonplace things like raising one's reading speed, playing a musical instrument better, and reducing one's golf handicap are included here. Usually, it's restricting filters that are causing issues. As a result, many of the methods applied to mental health applications would also be applicable here.

The Practitioner should elicit beliefs, values, and meta-programs to identify barriers and constraints. In the previous book in this series, I covered how modelling involves calibrating a subject's meta-programs. Here, too, the same method works. Additionally, watch out for opposing viewpoints and unfavourable anchors. A parts-integration technique would be necessary when the former happens. I would employ a collapsing anchor intervention for the latter. Allow me to go into further depth on collapsing anchors.

A perception that initiates a particular condition is called an anchor. Any one of the five modalities may witness this. If a particular scent brings back memories of your mother's perfume, it may create memories of her. Similarly, you will experience grief again if someone touches you on the shoulder during a funeral, and then later in the day, someone else touches you there. We refer to this as shooting an anchor.

One can purposefully install anchors. Words, touches, smells, or things your person sees may unintentionally become associated if they are experiencing a certain state. You are intentionally doing this as a Practitioner.

Here's an illustration. Let's say someone is extremely anxious right before an exam. You ask them to recall the previous instance of this happening. You say something or maybe give them a gentle tap on the right wrist when they reach what you believe to be their peak recall condition.

Next, disrupt the status quo by posing an unbiased query. Next, fire your anchor to check if you trigger the same situation.

After testing it and breaking the condition again, ask your subject to recall an instance in which they felt especially in control, self-assured, and at ease. When they are at their best, give them a gentle tap on the left wrist. Next, to break the state, let go of your anchor and pose a neutral question again.

After asking them to reconsider their study-related worry, touch them on the right wrist to establish the proper anchor. Touch them on their other wrist, their positive anchor, immediately after that. Release the negative anchor and observe the instantaneous shift in their state in a few seconds. You have unprogrammed their limiting filter and collapsed their negative anchor.

This is an illustration of a very basic self-improvement method. Naturally, I was describing a scenario in which a subject collaborated with a Practitioner in this case. There is not always a need for the second person. This is an independent technique that anyone can use.

Different Types of Deception

• Among other things, unintentional opposition to other people's demands might be lying, accusing others, sarcasm, and disguising anger.

• Allusive or implicit threats. One instance of this would be if you, as a mother, were to scold your child for leaving their unclean uniform on the ground.

• Characteristics such as lying, cheating, corruption, and even theft are examples of dishonesty.

- Selfishness in sharing important knowledge. For instance, let's say you have a friend in the same situation as you and withhold information regarding employment openings from them.
- She is forcing someone to quit a business or a group of close friends. This might apply to a single mother who separates her child from the father and his family, who genuinely cares for him out of spite for the father.
- Make an effort to undermine someone's convictions. Low self-esteem, denial, and misdirection are frequently the results of this.
- Insulting, condemning, or harshly criticizing criticizing someone else. Bullying is a common example.
- Reaching an objective through sex. Both employers and employees frequently do this.

Those who are being manipulated, however, may experience poor mental health if the manipulation is not handled. Prolonged manipulation can lead to poor coping strategies, anxiety, despair, dishonesty, and trouble trusting others. Additionally, it could cause a person to lose their sense of morality and start questioning everything. One such scenario was depicted in the iconic film Gaslight, in which a woman's spouse gently influences her until she stops depending on her perceptions. Subtly rejecting the gaslights, the guy led his wife to believe that the dimness of the light was all in her imagination.

Additionally, skilled at expressing charming things that their target would find appealing, manipulators often say things that are not entirely accurate. They use their expertise to form intimate and remarkable connections with people. A manipulator will purposefully set up an unbalanced situation to exploit their victim. Such a person will stop at nothing to acquire what they want.

When you see certain subtle behaviours, either in yourself or others, you should be wary of manipulation. Examples include being naive and consistently putting up a happy, charming front. To be honest, we all have engaged in manipulation at some point. Sometimes, you can lie to escape a predicament or even flatter someone to dominate them. For certain individuals, it's a way of life.

Manipulators are prevalent, as you may already be aware of or have firsthand knowledge of. What kind of personalities do they have should be the inquiry. Your next-door neighbour who gossips about you might be a manipulator. Someone could ultimately deceive you; they could even be members of your family who constantly cause upheaval or instil insecurity in others around them. When you're driving, manipulators are typically thieves who use tricks to divert your attention so they may steal your possessions.

Characteristics Of Preferential Manipulator Victims

People with Sensitivity

Manipulation includes power, but it doesn't simply include it. People who are sensitive and intelligent don't abuse their power to control others. When someone with more comparative power cannot achieve their goals through negotiation or other channels, they will typically resort to deceitful tactics, ultimately leading to manipulation.

You must worry about the other person's thoughts or feelings to counteract emotional manipulation. This counteracts the authority they possess over you. The ability to use external force to compel behaviour is not the same as emotional manipulation; if you think that the aggressor's denial of a request could cause physical injury, then this is a bigger issue than emotional manipulation and is outside the purview of this discussion. But it takes emotional manipulation to have the ability to force you from within. You now have two options. The first has the potential to weaken you or to show you that you are ultimately in charge of what happens inside of you. Never allow an outsider to control what occurs inside. In the end, only you possess the ability to control your fate. Therefore, you must develop the habit of keeping that in mind.

Those with Empathy

A person who absorbs emotions more than the average person is called an empathetic. They will be more sensitive to the slightest indication that the other person wants anything done for them, and they will proceed to fulfil that request to avoid feeling guilty. This does not imply that the other individual oversees the empath.

Evidence suggests that women tend to be softer and more empathetic than males. That's fine, but reminding someone that's who they are makes them adopt the preconceptions and makes them more susceptible to manipulation.

Being told that you are attractive, seductive, or beautiful can impair your intelligence in some way, which sets you up for exploitation. Not always, but it is possible. Men frequently lavish women with obeisance and praise to manipulate them. The reminder that they are women combined with the gifts and accolades is what breaks them, not the presents and praises.

Before the event, you should work on strengthening your mental state. It is comparable to constructing a mediaeval city's walls. You build the walls beforehand rather than waiting to erect them after the invading army arrives.

Changing your self-perception and gender stereotypes is another thing you need to do. When you neutralise it, it becomes more difficult for someone to use something against you. A small number of slave owners can nonetheless have control over hundreds of slaves if you study the art of enslavement. Why? Can't the slaves overwhelm them in quantity? No, since their mentality has yielded to manipulation and their frame of mind has been altered.

You can repel most manipulative aggressors if you guard your thoughts and mind.

Fear of Being Alone

A victim is more likely to experience love bombing and to experience it more intensely than other victims if they appear desperate, lonely, and in need of consolation. A less dramatic and perhaps more understated approach to the love bombing will be necessary if the victim is more grounded.

The theory behind love bombing is that it will instil in the victim a strong sense of devotion, trust, and cooperation with their manipulator. The manipulator's assessment of the circumstance typically determines the intensity of the love bombing and the target of the attack.

Fear of Letting Others Down

Let's say that your fears are making you believe unfavourable ideas, which will manifest as bad deeds. If so, your relationship may start to suffer from several negative impacts from your insecurity at that point. Even while it might not happen right away, know that it's acceptable to need help overcoming fears, whether it be from your partner's love and support, a therapist, or yourself.

DARK PSYCHOLOGY "Dark Psychology refers to the psychological nature of people to prey upon others driven by delusional, deviant, or psychologic criminal impulses that transcend intent and universal conclusions regarding instinctive forces, evolutionary biology, and social science theory. It is both a creation of human consciousness and an analysis of the human condition." Every person has the potential to victimise another person.

The study of dark psychology focuses on how people's psychological makeup makes them more likely to prey on others. Humanity as a whole can harm numerous people as well as other living things. While many people repress or sublimate these urges, others give in. The goal of dark psychology is to comprehend the thoughts, sentiments, and emotions that motivate predatory behaviour in people. Dark Psychology makes the 99.99 per cent assumption that this output is objective and motivated by some sort of rational, goal-oriented purpose. The remaining 0.01% falls under the category of Dark Psychology and refers to the willful victimisation of people without justification or a reasonable understanding of religion or scientific theories of evolution.

If not eradicated, predators and their violent, abusive, and fraudulent occurrences will become a global issue and a social crisis in the next century. The categories of predators include online sexual predators, cyberbullies, cyberterrorists, cybercriminals, computer stalkers, and political and religious anti-war zealots. iPredator's worldview, which encompasses aggression, harassment, and cyber victimisation through information and communications technology, fits the same paradigm as Dark Psychology, which views all illegal and deviant behaviour on a continuum of seriousness and motive. The following is the meaning of iPredator:

1. The Predator

A person, organisation, or country that uses information and communications technology (ICT) to exploit, victimise, coerce, stalk, steal from, or disqualify others is known as an iPredator. Deviant tendencies, the need for power and control, retaliation, political repression, religious fanaticism, mental illness, perceptual errors, social recognition, or the desire for both financial and personal fulfilment are the main causes of predators. Predators are not limited by national heritage, religion, race, or economic standing; they can be any gender or age. A global notion known as "iPredator" is used to define anyone who uses ICT in an abusive, deviant, manipulative, or criminal manner. The primary tenet of the development is that present psychologic categories of humanity consist of Information Age offenders, deviants, and physically unwell people.

iPredator can target anyone who engages in online child abuse, be it through a distributor or consumer of online defamation, cyberstalking, cyber harassment, cybercrime, online sexual predation, internet trolling, cyber extremism, cyberbullying, or malicious web manipulation. The following three standards were applied to define the iPredator:

Self-awareness regarding the potential for utilising ICT to damage others, whether directly or indirectly; the use of ICT to gather, disseminate, and transfer harmful knowledge.

A general definition of cyber stealth is the ability to track, identify, locate, monitor, and interact with an object or to engage in illicit or deviant activities.

Predators, as opposed to human predators living before the Information Age, depend on the numerous advantages of Information and Communication Technology [ICT]. This support entails speedy information sharing, long-distance information exchange, and seemingly limitless access to available data. Predators are malevolent individuals who use ICT in cyberspace's intricate and digital world to deceive others. Since the internet, by nature, provides anonymity to all ICT users, predators deliberately create online personas and employ deceptive strategies to evade detection and remain untraceable.

As a sub-tenet of iPredator, cyber stealth is a covert tool used by iPredators to establish and maintain total anonymity when they are involved in ICT operations to plan their next attack, investigate novel surveillance methods, or find the social media profiles of their next target. The concept of Cyberstealth is coupled with iPredator Victim Intuition [IVI]. This refers to iPredator's capacity to identify ODDOR [Offline Distress Dictates Online Response] objectives, technical constraints, psychological shortfalls, online and offline vulnerabilities, and their efficacy in cyberattacks with minimal consequences.

Taking Root

Using the anchoring approach, you can more closely identify with your joyful experiences, strong points, and positive feelings. When you link a modest gesture to a happy feeling, you'll notice that you're developing the habit to the point when the small act becomes a source of optimism.

● Determine whatever good feeling you are experiencing. Is it contentment, serenity, or self-assurance?

● Try to integrate this into your mindset by recalling a previous instance in which you had similar emotions.

● Boost the strength and clarity of the mental picture you are forming in your head.

● Select an anchoring word or gesture to establish a connection with this mental image now. "I am feeling ___" may serve as the anchoring statement. You might be contacting the back of your hand with the gesture.

● Repeat this at least once a day to help form a habit. Continue doing this until you can directly link the action or word to the emotion, causing your body and mind to light up.

● This well-practised anchoring method can be applied whenever you wish to shift your attitude to a more upbeat one.

Setting Up Accord

Using this effective NLP strategy, you can get along with everyone you meet. There are several strategies to establish rapport, but the simplest and most fundamental is to mimic the other person's body language, facial emotions, and breathing rhythm. Finding out the predominant sensory perception of the other person is another method for establishing rapport. Is it visual, aural, or kinesthetic? Once you've recognised this, you can also reflect this. Phrases like "I feel nice about this" or "I feel that is incorrect" exemplify how kinesthetic perception is articulated. Expressions of auditory perception include "I hear you" and "I'm listening." Expressions like "I can see your idea" or "I can see where you are coming from" are used by those who have visual perception.

Shifting Beliefs

Overcoming conditioned, limiting beliefs can be a difficult endeavour. Concentrating on the advantages rather than the drawbacks of any given circumstance is one of the finest strategies for altering your views. Let's say, for instance, that you are having trouble working with your boss even though everyone else is getting along with him. Reflect on past supervisors you enjoyed working with and see if you can apply what you learned to this situation.

A daily practice of affirmations can also help you shift your beliefs. For instance, if you're hoping to change careers, say these affirmations aloud each morning: "I will find a great job that I will be very happy with." These positive affirmations can transform your body and mind into a positive space, inspiring you to put in more effort and land that dream job.

As you may have noticed, many of these NLP strategies were used in the well-known ones covered in the first two chapters. See the magic these methods may work for you when you incorporate them into your daily life.

The thing that you make it with is NLP.

In the unlikely event that you apply NLP to enhance your interpersonal skills, then that's NLP - for you.

In the unlikely event, the same holds true if you utilise it to empower your children and help them develop confidence.

Becoming a more proficient holistic mentor

Promote goods or services, either ethically or dishonestly

Expand your company or strengthen your administrative skills

Attract attention from others. Be a charismatic leader

Become a more and more effective expert

Improve in the sport you have chosen.

Con people out of their money

Encourage the people you live or work with by helping them overcome their worries.

Boost your performance as a teacher

Participate in your community

Get better at b-ball, cruising, golfing, and other activities. Become a better friend to yourself or others.

It determines what NLP specifically signifies for you and what you receive in return, regardless of how and for what purpose you utilise it.

Here are a few publications that explore the application of NLP in diverse life domains:

The executives

NLP is a close-to-essential tool for utilising and adapting to the changes in today's director or group pioneer work.

Life Guidance, Mentoring, Evaluation, And Therapy

NLP emerged from the study of effective therapy and is the ideal complement to almost any teaching or healing approach. At Pegasus, we have firsthand experience with Clean Communication using NLP to assist people in a way that gives them the confidence to find solutions independently.

Regarding interpersonal relationships, NLP enables us to communicate with others more effectively by helping us understand what it's like to be them. Thus, it's great for moving forward, making relationships at home and in social situations and persevering.

Your internal existence

We are exposed to many amazing skills and information at school, including maths, science, history, craftsmanship, and more. Nevertheless, the missing component—for instance, detailed guidance on handling your reflections and mental states—is really important. One of the most important uses of NLP is for self-improvement and personal development.

Purchasing

A skilled salesperson understands that relationships, repeat business and well-crafted proposals are what lead to success in the long run and establish you as the go-to supplier. NLP skills enable you to enhance your ability to Develop generally beneficial relationships with clients, Identify their needs and inspiration, and Coordinate objects with inspiration.

Vocational advancement used to be sufficient to be approved at your employment. That has been modified. These days, you also need to be a gifted communicator, possess the ability to inspire and connect with colleagues, and possess the ability to market and sell oneself. This is where NLP aptitudes are useful.

Play

Nowadays, it is widely accepted that mental attitude plays a fundamentally important role in sports. Therefore, whether you are an eager novice or an exceptional athlete, You can use NLP tools to give yourself the upper hand.

The many applications of natural language

Many find the range of applications for natural language processing (NLP) astounding, if not confusing.

It seems strange that the same process might help you enhance your relationships with friends and family, your professional performance, your tennis or golf game, and your ability to help your child learn to read and write.

However, as you will quickly discover while using NLP, there are no genuinely limitless applications for NLP, nor are there areas of your life that cannot benefit from it.

Rather than providing specific skills to achieve certain goals, it offers the means to enhance your overall sufficiency. (for example, a reflection approach to quiet yourself or a confidence strategy for transmitting). This makes it extremely beneficial.

Do whatever you can to improve right now!

With NLP, you learn to think about developing and improving rather than "fixing issues." Instead of trying to force anything to work, you learn how to look for new and increasingly creative methods to deal with life's challenges.

Chapter 7: How can I stay motivated and disciplined all the time?

Everybody has dreams. Those we discuss and those we keep private. To achieve our objectives, we require great bravery and self-assurance. Everything is up to us and what we do. Of course, there are ups and downs, but pursuing the objective consistently is what matters most.

Visualizations are useful in situations like these. They are like dreams in that we let our imagination run wild without worrying about any constraints at this point. This is the main idea behind visualization: it is a self-improvement strategy that directs our thoughts towards our objectives and aspirations. It modifies attitudes towards the objective or target and affects thoughts and feelings. An action-ready state is already within your reach! It is crucial to appeal to all senses since the more aroma, colour, sound, and texture an imagination can create, the more vividly and powerfully you can recall it.

The submodalities—distinctive qualities of images produced by the senses that heighten the feeling—should be mentioned in this context. In visualization, these could be considered the boundaries of cognition.

Submodalities enable you to intentionally mould and shape your thoughts, giving you more control over their essence. You will be free of ideas that appear out of nowhere and spread unfavourable feelings. They will be swiftly replaced with pictures of confident, uplifting scenarios inspiring you to work towards your goals. Your thoughts might already start to become more colourful and mindful. You can utilize this technique to modify your limiting experience by lessening it and to conjure scenarios that offer you power when you strengthen them even more with various sensory experiences.

Developing motivation and self-control also entails decreasing your unpleasant feelings, forcing you to reduce the range of your sensory experiences to the point where they are little and grey till they vanish, or at the very least, they will have less of an effect on your thoughts. If you examine it more closely, you will see that it is worthwhile to back up your beliefs since, in actuality, motivation and self-control begin with ourselves and require a shift in perspective. Don't let bad memories hold you back or sap your vitality. Maintain a constant state of motivation by creating a positive thought and event collection, like a photo album to which you can refer. This will keep you in a positive frame of mind and give you the energy and inspiration to help others grow. Because it functions somewhat like a mechanism that you must film, once it is gone, it is sufficient to keep you motivated at all times, to cultivate your ideas, and to take care of creating new ones about what the future should hold to continually pursue your objectives and realize your aspirations.

Unfortunately, developing self-discipline and motivation needs repetition and focus. However, you may make the process easier and more lasting by working on yourself with NLP techniques like modelling, anchoring, or visualization. Not only that, but regular visualization production also contributes to maintaining motivation. It also impacts how we view the past, feel about our future aspirations, and how eager we are to carry out our decisions. The biggest shifts in our lives come from how we view reality, everything around us, and ourselves. They also come from a desire to comprehend other people's motivations and behaviours.

Since we frequently truly enjoy accomplishment with our closest family members, maintaining positive relationships with friends and family, forging strong bonds with business associates, and maintaining an optimistic outlook on life are all crucial components of motivation. Positive energy rebounds from others, and bad energy reflects on ourselves. Though you can never be too helpful, kindness and a smile never fail to please our clients. Modelling is a key component of motivation; in this case, it also occurs when you meet and become acquainted with others who will motivate you, teach you new things, and provide you with an example of successful patterns to follow. Recall that surroundings matter. It's preferable to follow admirable people who pursue success than to be around whiny, lazy people who blame everyone else for their misdeeds. You can control your life today and make the most out of it in terms of happiness, fulfilment, and plain old fun.

Regular practice of visualizations is recommended because our brains retain precise and distinctive images better when stimulated in an organized manner that involves all of our senses and meticulous attention to detail. Items and particular occasions are also simpler to remember, and habits are formed by doing them repeatedly.

Submodalities can also enhance such visualizations. Don't place restrictions on yourself. Imagine a grand panorama that is bright and colourful, next to you, audible and sufficiently energetic. Reversing this approach will assist you in suppressing the events and visions you wish to eliminate: the shrinking image, the grey, calm, and remote. One helpful component that will help your visualizations is affirmations. Repeating your goal aloud in your vision or the words themselves will provide you with drive and strength when visualizing a scene representing the event you want to achieve. To help your brain retain the image, making your sensory experiences more intense is crucial.

Recall! Your subconscious becomes active when you consistently apply conscious mental influence to the task. Prepare your mind for success by starting today. Don't let other people, the media, the internet, or television dictate your aspirations. If your goals are unmet, you become an employee of others, realizing others' aspirations rather than your own. Perhaps there is something worth changing?

What Is Dark Psychology, Chapter 1?

Dark psychology can be broadly defined as the science and art of manipulating and controlling the mind. This phenomenon characterizes people's strategies and methods to influence, persuade, coerce, and inspire others. While some employ dark psychology methods for charitable purposes, another subset does so for personal benefit. Along with learning constructive applications of dark psychology, we must recognize the telltale signs of self-serving individuals and know how to steer clear of them. Psychologists and criminologists claim that most individuals who use dark psychology for self-serving purposes exhibit particular behaviours known as "The dark triad."

Narcissism, psychopathy, and Machiavellianism comprise the "dark psychology triad." Narcissism is typified by grandiosity, egoism, and, most importantly, a lack of empathy.
Although charm and friendliness are traits of psychopathy, the true nature of the trait is one of hidden selfish agenda, lack of empathy, impulsivity, and complete lack of regret.

Nobody wants to be taken advantage of or manipulated, but it happens to us occasionally. Dark psychology ignorance makes us susceptible to manipulation. Even if you have never been the victim of someone who matches the dark triad, you nevertheless encounter people in everyday life who use one or both of these strategies to acquire what they want from you.

It may surprise you that certain bosses' behaviours, online advertisements, and sales practices all employ some of these strategies.

If you are a parent, particularly of young children or teenagers, you are undoubtedly familiar with their strategies to coerce you into doing things. Many youngsters experiment with some of the dark psychology methods in an attempt to gain control or get what they want. Most individuals you love and trust are the ones who utilize subtle manipulation and dark persuasion. As unbelievable as it may seem, those familiar with you are more likely than strangers to employ these coercive tactics since they know just which buttons to push. Common manipulative strategies employed by ordinary people include deception, choice restriction, withdrawal, love flooding, love denial, and reverse psychology.

Giving someone options but diverting their attention from the decision you do not want them to make is known as choice limitation. When someone uses a choice restriction, they typically set a time limit for you to examine your options, ask for your response as soon as possible, and ensure you don't give it much thought.

Avoiding the individual and treating them silently are examples of withdrawal. This method typically helps those who are attention-seeking and dependent on other people's acceptance, as well as those who are terrified of being alone.

Withholding affection and attention from a certain person is known as love denial.

The tactic known as "love flooding" is showering someone with praise, affection, or even physical abuse to get them to comply with our requests.

In reverse psychology, you instruct the other person to do what you truly desire.

Telling lies includes:

Suppressing the truth.

Stating only parts of the truth.

Keeping and exaggerating certain details.

To confuse someone, semantic manipulation is using terms that have similar meanings (create the impression of being misunderstood.). When someone uses this tactic, they typically retract their statements later on. Words have a great deal of power.

While some individuals intentionally employ dark psychology strategies for their benefit, others do so without realizing what they are doing. Some people unconsciously adopt dark and unethical means to get what they want. The majority of those who inadvertently employ dark psychology learn the practice from their parents and other early influences. Since they have been using these methods since they were young, the users consider it normal. Some pick up these habits as teenagers or adults. Some people picked up these talents by accident. For example, they tried something, and it worked well for them; as a result, they began utilizing it often but subconsciously.

Certain individuals have received professional training on how to employ these strategies. For example, most marketers and salespeople employ some form of dark psychology to attract customers. Most programmes that typically employ dark persuasion techniques are sales and marketing. In essence, these programmes seek to draw clients for their selfish ends rather than using dark psychology to assist the client. It's interesting to note that the programme persuades its students that using dark psychology is OK because the buyer is the ultimate recipient of the goods they have purchased. At some time, the skilled manipulator is also taken advantage of.

What Does a Hypnotherapist Get Train in?

For some, hypnotherapy might mean taking a risk or, better yet, finding out more about their hypnotherapist's background and how to support them. Despite the lack of an official hypnotherapy programme offered by an approved university or college, healthcare practitioners have acquired knowledge of this gaining popularity and incorporated it into their training repertoire. Physicians, dentists, social workers, master nurses, psychologists, and family and marital therapists are among the medical professionals who have received hypnosis training.

Five Intentions For Hypnosis

Hypnotherapy has a broad range of applications in treating mental, emotional, and physical health issues. Health practitioners frequently recommend hypnotherapy for patients or clients experiencing acute or unexpected illnesses, as well as persistent pain and sadness.

Anyone thinking about hypnosis can benefit from carefully studying the following five hypnotic applications:

1. Handling of Fears and Fears

An unjustified or irrational fear of nearly anything is known as a phobia. Individuals battle with these issues daily. This crippling terror often paralyses them. Arachnophobia, or the fear of spiders; claustrophobia, or the dread of enclosed spaces, snakes, heights, flying, and leaving the house are common fears among those who suffer from phobias. We refer to this as a phobia.

Hypnotherapists employ hypnosis to help patients identify potential triggers for their concerns and diligently seek out answers.

2. Give Up Smoking

When smokers are prepared to give up smoking completely, they frequently need to take stronger steps. No matter how much a smoker wants to stop, it usually takes several tries before they can completely give up cigarettes and nicotine. Hypnotists in the medical field can assist their patients by fostering a calm environment and attempting to identify the stressors in their lives that may lead to relapses in smoking during periods of conscious quitting.

3. Weight-Loss Equipment

Sometimes, those who are trying to lose weight feel like their lives are spinning out of control. Even if they wish to have a positive perspective on food, a trained hypnotherapist can assist clients in understanding their relationship with food and the reasons behind the intense symptoms of obsessive-compulsive disorder.

4. Booster of Confidence

Many people struggle with self-confidence and frequently require unbiased assistance to grow. Sometimes, a significant life transition is necessary to boost someone's confidence, like going on a job interview or looking for a new romantic partner. Making the most of and accurately identifying their best traits is something a trained hypnotherapist can assist clients with.

5. Anesthesiology in Surgery

Surgeons occasionally employ hypnotherapists to support anaesthesia. ASCH's study indicates that hypnotherapy has occasionally been the only anaesthetic used during surgical procedures. Additionally, hypnosis has been employed by surgeons during hysterectomy, caesarean section, amputation, and cholecystectomy procedures. Without hypnotism, it would be impossible for patients to undergo life-saving and health-improving procedures if they are allergic to or sensitive to chemicals used during anaesthesia.

www.ingramcontent.com/pod-product-compliance
Lightning Source LLC
Chambersburg PA
CBHW052157110526
44591CB00012B/1989